KNOW YOUR BODY

YOUR LUNGS

By George Fittleworth

Gareth Stevens
PUBLISHING

Please visit our website, www.garethstevens.com. For a free color catalog of all our high-quality books, call toll free 1-800-542-2595 or fax 1-877-542-2596.

Library of Congress Cataloging-in-Publication Data

Fittleworth, George, author.
 Your lungs / George Fittleworth.
     pages cm.
 Includes bibliographical references and index.
 ISBN 978-1-4824-4456-8 (pbk.)
 ISBN 978-1-4824-4400-1 (6 pack)
 ISBN 978-1-4824-4437-7 (library binding)
 1. Lungs—Juvenile literature. 2. Respiratory organs—Juvenile literature. 3. Human physiology—Juvenile literature. I. Title.
 QP121.F58 2017
 612.2′4—dc23

                           2015021478

Published in 2017 by
Gareth Stevens Publishing
111 East 14th Street, Suite 349
New York, NY 10003

Copyright © 2017 Gareth Stevens Publishing

Designer: Andrea Davison-Bartolotta
Editor: Therese Shea

Photo credits: Cover, p. 1 Sergey Novikov/Shutterstock.com; pp. 3, 4, 6, 8, 10, 12, 14, 16, 18, 20, 22–24 Anna Frajtova/Shutterstock.com; p. 5 Sebastian Kaulitzki/Shutterstock.com; p. 7 wxin/iStock/Thinkstock; p. 9 (main) Jovanmandic/iStock/Thinkstock; p. 9 (inset) Alil MedicalMedia/Shutterstock.com; pp. 11, 13 (lungs) decade3d - anatomy online/Shutterstock.com; p. 13 (main) Andrea Danti/Shutterstock.com; p. 13 (background) MaxyM/Shutterstock.com; p. 15 (main) Jupiterimages/Creatas/Thinkstock; p. 15 (inset) Designua/Shutterstock.com; p. 17 Wavebreakmedia Ltd/Wavebreak Media/Thinkstock; p. 19 Westend61/Getty Images; p. 21 Fotokostic/Shutterstock.com.

Printed in the United States of America

CPSIA compliance information: Batch #CS16GS: For further information contact Gareth Stevens, New York, New York at 1-800-542-2595.

CONTENTS

Boldface words appear in the glossary.

Locating the Lungs

Take a deep breath. Now breathe out. You couldn't live without breathing. You couldn't breathe or live without your lungs! You have two lungs in your chest. The one on the left is a little smaller, so there's room for your heart.

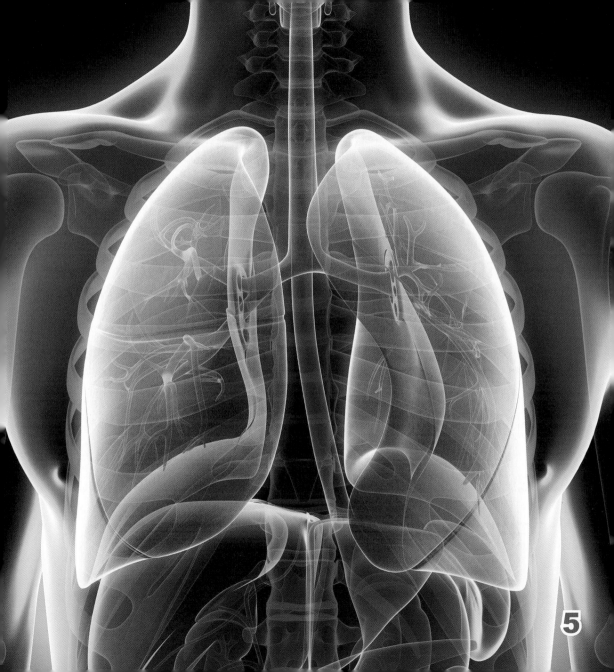
5

What They Do

You breathe in a gas the body needs called oxygen. You breathe out a waste gas called carbon dioxide. The lungs work with many other body parts to make this happen. Together, they're called the respiratory (REHS-peh-reh-tor-ee) system.

oxygen

carbon dioxide

Breathing In

Each lung rests on a sheet of **muscle** called the diaphragm (DY-uh-fram). It helps the lungs fill with air and empty. When you breathe in through your nose or mouth, the air goes in a tube called the trachea (TRAY-kee-ah).

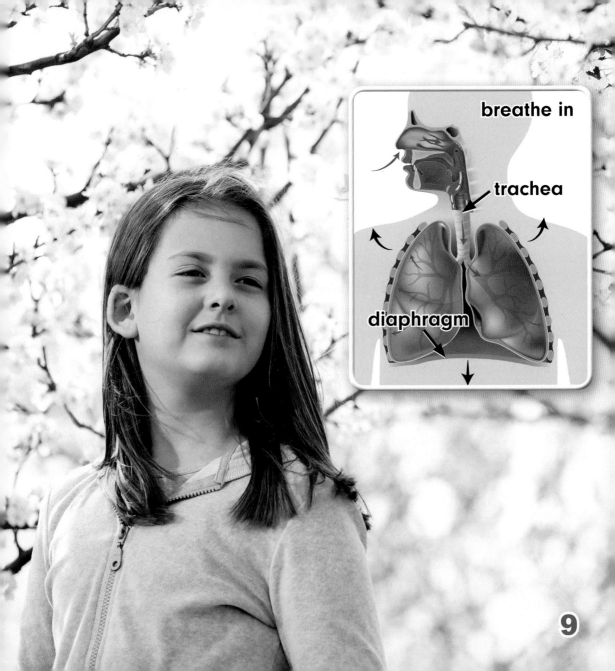

breathe in

trachea

diaphragm

9

The trachea connects to two tubes called the bronchi (BRAHN-kee). Each of these tubes leads to one of the lungs and to smaller tubes called bronchioles (BRAHN-kee-ohlz). Bronchioles lead to tiny **sacs** called alveoli (al-VEE-oh-lee).

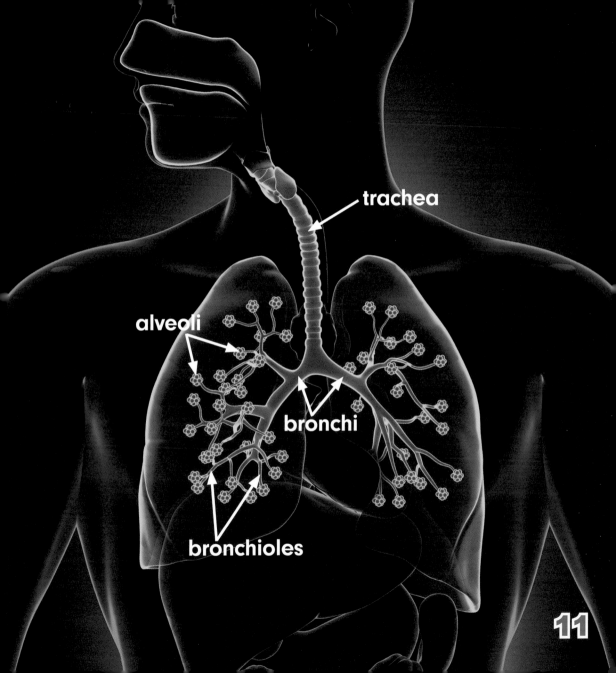

trachea

alveoli

bronchi

bronchioles

11

Each sac is covered by tiny **blood vessels** carrying blood that needs oxygen. The alveoli allow oxygen to pass through their thin walls and enter the blood. Blood with oxygen goes to the heart, which **pumps** it throughout the body.

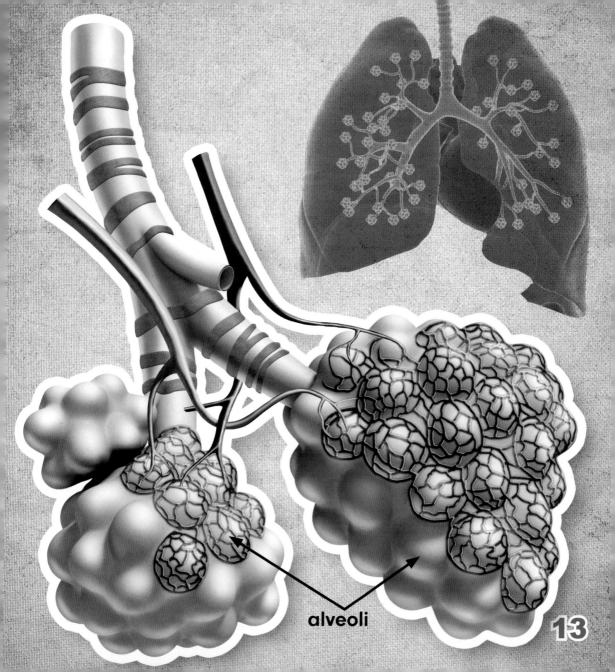

alveoli

13

Oxygen for Life

Every cell in your whole body needs oxygen to live. Every cell also needs to get rid of waste. The blood that receives oxygen also lets go of its carbon dioxide. This waste gas goes into the alveoli.

oxygen

carbon dioxide

alveolar wall

blood vessel

red blood cells

AIR

CO_2

O_2

carbon dioxide out

oxygen in

Breathing Out

When you breathe out, everything happens in **reverse**. The waste air leaves the alveoli and goes out the bronchioles, the bronchi, and the trachea. You let it out through your mouth and nose. Then, it happens all over again!

breathe out

diaphragm

It's a Trap!

Your lungs are lined with sticky **mucus** that can trap harmful things you breathe in, such as **germs** and bits of dust. You breathe or **cough** out these things so they don't stay in your body.

Love Your Lungs

Luckily, you don't have to remember to breathe. Your brain makes sure you do it, even when you're sleeping. You can do things to keep your lungs healthy, such as exercising and staying away from smoke. Love your lungs!

GLOSSARY

blood vessel: a small tube in your body that carries blood

cough: to force air through your throat with a short, loud noise

germ: a tiny living thing that can cause illness

mucus: a thick slime produced by the bodies of many animals

muscle: one of the parts of the body that allow movement

pump: to force a liquid, such as water, through a space

reverse: to move in the opposite direction

sac: a part inside the body that is shaped like a bag and usually contains liquid or air

FOR MORE INFORMATION

BOOKS

Bailey, Jacqui. *What Happens When You Breathe?* New York, NY: PowerKids Press, 2009.

Burstein, John. *The Remarkable Respiratory System: How Do My Lungs Work?* New York, NY: Crabtree Publishing, 2009.

Hewitt, Sally. *My Heart and Lungs.* Laguna Hills, CA: QEB Publishing, 2008.

WEBSITES

Your Lungs
www.cyh.com/HealthTopics/HealthTopicDetailsKids. aspx?id=2406&np=152&p=335
Read about what happens when the lungs have problems.

Your Lungs and Respiratory System
kidshealth.org/kid/htbw/lungs.html#
Find out much more about lungs on this site.

INDEX

KNOW YOUR BODY

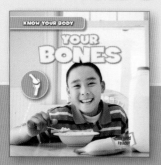

YOUR BONES

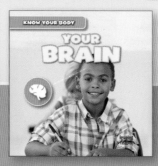

YOUR BRAIN

YOUR HEART

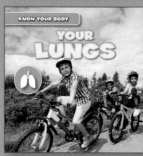

YOUR LUNGS

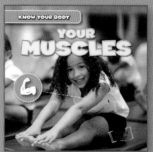

YOUR MUSCLES

YOUR STOMACH

Levels: GR: K; DRA: 20

ISBN: 978-1-4824-4456-8
6-pack ISBN: 978-1-4824-4400-1

9 781482 444568

Gareth Stevens
PUBLISHING